MELANIE & CHRIS RICE

ALL ABOUT THINGS PEOPLE DO

Illustrated by
Lesley Smith

TAXI 675

Kingfisher Books

Contents

All around

People are busy everywhere, in towns and cities, in the countryside and at sea, even under the ground.

farming

collecting the rubbish

fishing

mining

People are busy at home and at work . . .

. . . helping out . . .

. . . and having fun.

Drivers

Drivers take people and their belongings from one place to another.

bus driver

taxi driver

rickshaw wallah

lorry driver

Here are some of the people who work at an airport.

A ground stewardess checks passenger tickets.

A baggage handler takes suitcases to the plane.

Ground engineers refuel the plane.

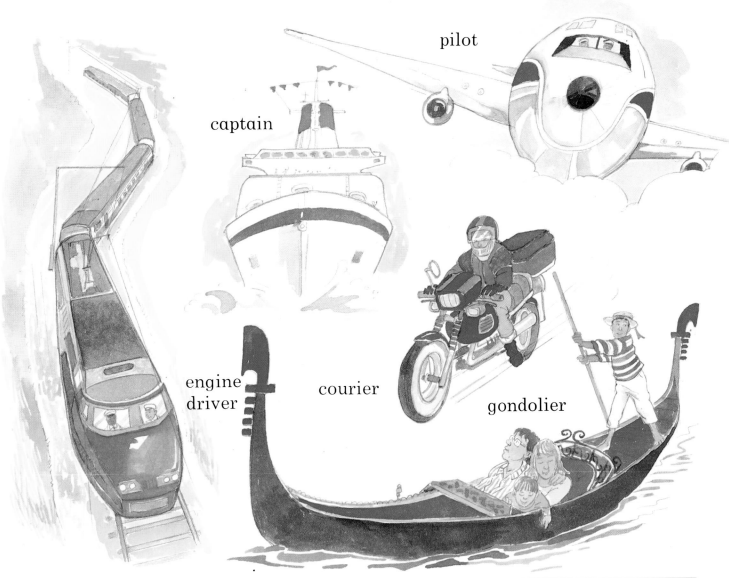

pilot

captain

engine
driver

courier

gondolier

A flight engineer
makes sure the plane
is ready to fly.

A stewardess looks
after the passengers.

An air traffic
controller guides the
pilot for take-off.

In the factory

In a car factory people work alongside robots and computers. Each person concentrates on just one part of the assembly line.

1 Before work begins, the design engineer draws up plans and models are tested.

4 The windscreens are sealed in place before the fitters lower the body onto its engine.

5 Then the insides of the car and its wheels are added. At every stage, supervisors check production standards.

2 Fitters position the side panels for the robots to weld together.

3 After the fitters hang the doors and bonnets on their hinges, robots spray the body of the car with paint.

6 Technicians test the car to make sure that everything works perfectly.

7 When people and machines work together, they can produce hundreds of cars each day.

Hands at work

Craftsmen and women, such as this basket weaver, make things by hand. People admire hand-crafted things because they take time and skill to make.

The potter shapes a pot from wet clay on a potter's wheel.

When the pot is dry he hardens it in a hot kiln.

When the pot is cold he decorates it with paint and glaze and fires it again in the kiln.

Be a potter

Mould your own pot, using modelling clay that hardens without heat.
Mark a pattern with an old spoon or fork.
When the pot is hard you can paint it in bright colours.

Carpenters cut and join wood using the tools in their workshop.

Glassblowers blow and twist hot glass into shapes which harden as they cool.

This watchmaker is checking tiny parts with a magnifying lens.

Builders

On construction sites many people work together. Before the builders begin, designers, architects and engineers discuss and plan the best way to carry out the job.

Building a tunnel   **Building a bridge**   **Building a road**

The designer must make the tunnel strong enough to hold back earth and water.

Engineers make sure the bridge will stand up to wind, waves and heavy traffic.

The surveyor measures the land so that the road will be straight and smooth.

A ship is designed on computers and tested with models before it is built in the shipyard.

Each section is constructed in an assembly hall and rolled out to the building dock.

A crane driver lifts the sections.

A welder joins them together.

A painter sprays over the joins.

Doing repairs

All the things we use, no matter how well they are made, need maintaining to stay in good order. When they break or go wrong they have to be repaired. Have you seen these people at work?

plumber

electrician

painter

window cleaner

road worker

telephone engineer

Mechanics work in a garage, servicing and mending cars.

A tool box

People need all kinds of tools to help them with their work. Who uses these tools?

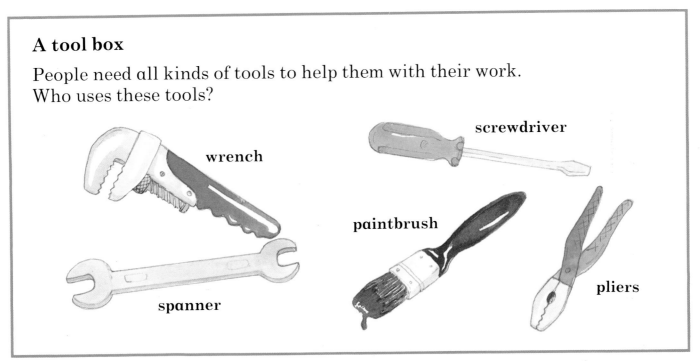

wrench

screwdriver

spanner

paintbrush

pliers

Making clothes

People make clothes at home, in small workshops and factories, by hand and with machines.

a hand-knitted jumper

a handmade hat

machine-made gymshoes

Here are some of the people who produced this cotton T-shirt.

A harvester gathered the cotton.

A spinner spun the cotton into thread.

A knitter wove the threads into material.

Be a designer

You need some paper, pencils, an old T-shirt and fabric crayons.

Draw your design on a piece of paper. Copy it onto the front of your T-shirt and colour it in with fabric crayons.

Ask an adult to cover the picture with paper or cloth and to iron over it. The heat will fix the colours.

A dyer coloured the material.

A designer sketched the T-shirt.

A machinist sewed up the material.

In the shops

We go shopping to buy the things we need. Shop assistants help us to find what we want and take our money at the till. They also fill the shelves and arrange displays.

Can you find these people?

shop assistant   fishmonger   grocer

The Hot Bread Shop

At the hairdresser

Some shops sell services, not goods.

Hairdressers are trained to wash and cut their customers' hair.

23

The customers choose from the
menu. The chef cooks their meal.

Waiters bring the
food to the table.

At the restaurant

People eat at a restaurant when they are too busy to cook their own meals or when they want a treat.

Can you see someone washing up?

You can buy ready-to-eat snacks in the street as well.

American hot-dogs

Italian ice-cream

Nigerian sweetcorn

Entertainers

Entertainers try to make their audience happy. They make them think too. Which entertainers do you enjoy watching most?

clown

magician

singer

musicians

Writers and illustrators entertain us with their books. But we do not watch them at work.

folk dancer

ballet dancers

circus acrobat

At the theatre

People come to the theatre to see the actors and musicians, but others are at work behind the scenes.

The director leads the rehearsals.

Scenic artists paint the sets for the stage.

The wardrobe mistress sews the costumes.

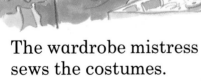

Sound and lighting technicians operate the sound and light effects.

29

Sport

Sport is enjoyed by people everywhere. Some like to take part, others prefer to watch.

jogging

skiing

sailing

swimming

basketball

People compete against each other . . .

. . . and play together in teams.

athletics

We can watch sport live
and at home on television.

snooker

A sports bag
Which sports need these?

skis

life jacket

track shoes

cue

basket

Working with animals

Animals are trained to help people with all kinds of work.

Oxen help a farmer to plough the land.

Guide dogs help blind people.

A team of huskies drags a sledge across the snow.

A camel carries a load across the desert.

An elephant moves heavy timber.

Animals everywhere
need to be cared for.

A vet is an animal
doctor.

A farrier shoes horses
and ponies.

Wardens protect wild animals
in parks and nature reserves.

The zookeeper makes sure that his
animals are clean and well fed.

To the rescue

The emergency services help people in danger. Firefighters, ambulance workers and police are hard at work at this fire.

Other people help out too.

health visitor

minister

neighbour

friend

Coastguards have called lifeboat and helicopter crews to the rescue.

In hospital

Day and night, doctors and nurses care for their patients in hospital. Receptionists, porters, cooks and cleaners all work hard behind the scenes.

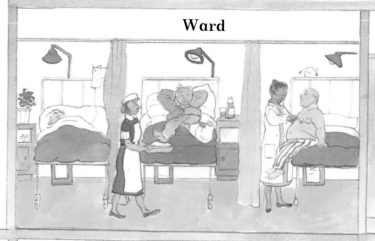

Ward

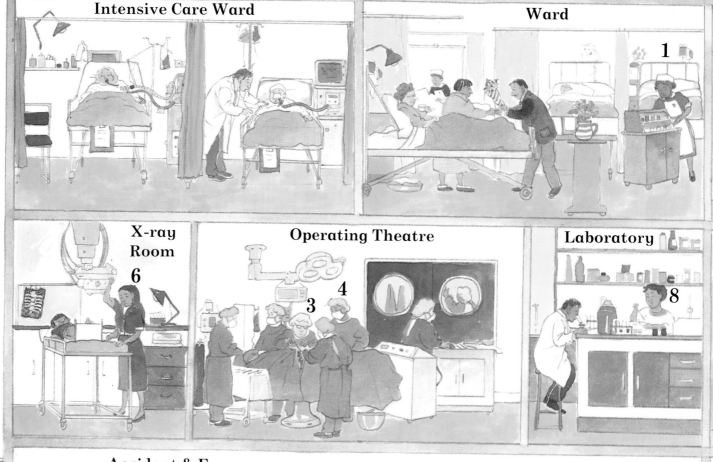

Intensive Care Ward

Ward

X-ray Room

Operating Theatre

Laboratory

Accident & Emergency

Reception

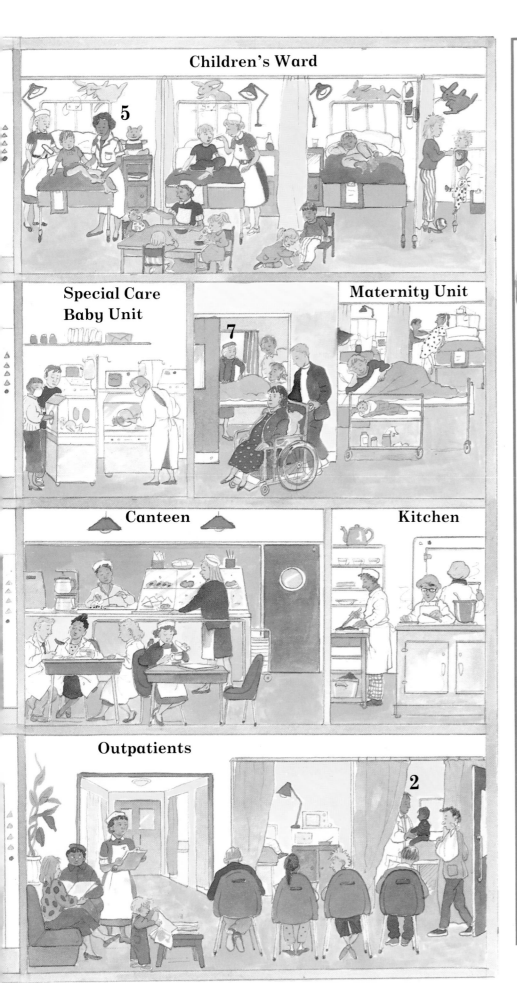

Children's Ward

5

Special Care Baby Unit

7

Maternity Unit

Canteen

Kitchen

Outpatients

2

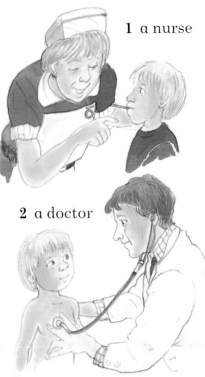

1 a nurse

2 a doctor

3 a surgeon in the Operating Theatre

4 a theatre nurse

5 a physiotherapist

6 a radiographer in the X-ray Room

7 a midwife in the Maternity Unit

8 a pharmacist in the Laboratory

9 a telephone operator in Reception

10 an ambulance worker in Accident & Emergency

Scientists

Scientists try to find out more about how our world works. There are many kinds of scientists doing research. They set themselves questions and conduct experiments to test their answers.

Some scientists look for cures for diseases.

Some try to find new ways of growing food.

Some search for clues that tell us more about the past.

Some investigate the sea bed . . .

. . . and some explore remote parts of the world.

Astronauts travel to space in rockets.

They do tests and bring back information which might be useful to us on Earth.

Astronomers study stars in the sky.

Try this experiment
What happens to sugar in water? Add some sugar to a glass of water and stir it.

Watch. The sugar disappears and becomes part of the water. It dissolves.

At school

These children are busy learning with their teachers at school.

Aa apple
Bb boat
Cc cat
Dd dog

The first people we learn from
are our parents. As we grow up,
teachers can tell us more about
the things that interest us.

music teacher

museum guide

librarian

medical professor

sports trainer

Bringing the news

We can find out what people are doing wherever they are.

We can ask them by making a phone call.

Telephone operators and engineers help us to keep in touch.

They can tell us in a letter or a postcard.

A postman delivers a postcard.

Reporters and photographers go out and meet people. Their stories are printed in newspapers and magazines for us to read.

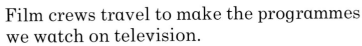

Film crews travel to make the programmes we watch on television.

Radio presenters broadcast the news from their studio.

Busy people day and night

The Corner Shop   10

The Corner Shop   10

CLOSED

Index